19.97

EXPLORING MUSIC

Woodwinds

Alyn Shipton

RSVP
RAINTREE
STECK-VAUGHN
PUBLISHERS
The Steck-Vaughn Company

Austin, Texas

Titles in the Series
Brass
Keyboards and Electronic Music
Percussion
Singing
Strings
Woodwinds

Consultant: Skipp Tullen
Editor: Pauline Tait
Picture Researcher: Suzanne Williams
Designer: Julian Holland
Illustrator: Lawrie Taylor, Terry Hadler
Electronic Production: Scott Melcer

Picture acknowledgments

Raintree Steck-Vaughn Publishers would like to thank the following photographic
sources: Edgarley Hall School music department, especially Mr. Brian Armfield, for
assistance with commissioned photography; and David Titchener for supplying the
photographs.

The author and publishers wish to thank the following photographic sources: Stuart
Chorley: copy of a chalumeau by J.C. Denner made by Brian Ackerman p16; The
Bridgeman Art Library, Denis van Alsloot (1570-c. 1626) *Detail from a Procession.*
Private Collection: p24; C.M. Dixon: p13 (right); The Hutchison Library: front
cover, p14 (bottom): Japan Information and Cultural Centre: p14 (top left); Mary
Evans Picture Library: p11 (left); Performing Arts Library/Clive Barda: p5, p18 (top
& bottom), p26; Redferns: p21/Mike Hutson, p22; Tumi *Latin American Craft
Centres* : p11/Mo Fini; Zefa: p29 (top left).

Cover credits
(Kenny G) © John Atashian/Retna;
(symphony) Performing Arts Library/Clive Barda

Library of Congress Cataloging-in-Publication Data

Shipton, Alyn.
    Woodwinds / Alyn Shipton.
       p.   cm. — (Exploring music)
    Includes index.
    Summary: Text and pictures introduce the woodwind family of instruments,
such as flutes, saxophones, oboes, bassoons, and their relatives.
    ISBN 0-8114-2319-0
    1. Woodwind instruments — Juvenile literature.   [1. Woodwind —
instuments.]   I. Title.   II. Series: Shipton, Alyn. Exploring music.
ML931.S53   1994
788.2'19—dc20   93-20224
                                      CIP
                                   MN AC

Printed and bound in the United States
1 2 3 4 5 6 7 8 9 0 VHP 99 98 97 96 95 94 93

Contents

Families of Instruments

In the modern orchestra, there is a woodwind section made up of a common group of instrumental families — flutes and piccolos, clarinets and saxophones, oboes and bassoons. Rarer instruments usually belong to one of these families — the English horn is a kind of oboe, and the basset horn is similar to a clarinet. The recorder used to be played with orchestras, but its place has now been taken by the modern flute except in "early music" **ensembles**. These ensembles play music of the past as it was played when it was written. In this book we meet each of the families in turn, as well as some similar instruments from the past, or from around the world, that do not form part of the orchestra.

Many of the instruments in the woodwind family that are played today are not made of wood. They can be made of metals, such as brass and silver, or other materials, such as horn, bone, or plastic.

The sizes of different instruments in a family are usually named after the ranges of the human voice. They range from **soprano** at the highest pitch to **bass** at the lowest, although there are sometimes minute "sopranino" versions, and sometimes vast and difficult to manage double, or "contra," bass instruments. Some instrumental families, like the saxophone, were invented to have all the voices, while others have only some.

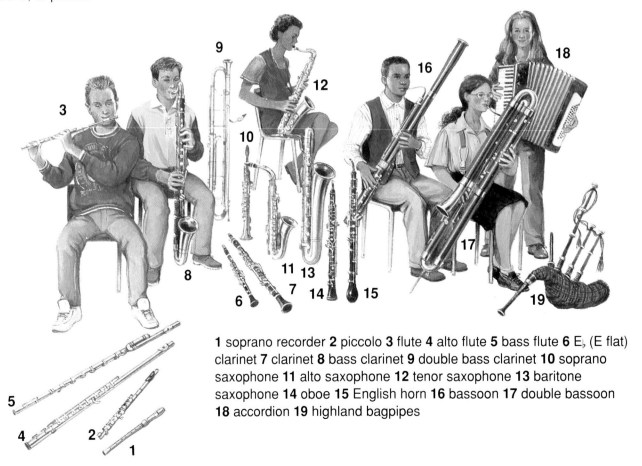

1 soprano recorder 2 piccolo 3 flute 4 alto flute 5 bass flute 6 E♭ (E flat) clarinet 7 clarinet 8 bass clarinet 9 double bass clarinet 10 soprano saxophone 11 alto saxophone 12 tenor saxophone 13 baritone saxophone 14 oboe 15 English horn 16 bassoon 17 double bassoon 18 accordion 19 highland bagpipes

Sound

When an object vibrates, it makes a sound. You hear the sound when the vibration passing through the air reaches your ear. As something vibrates, it pushes or pulls the air near it and sets up sound waves. These sound waves travel somewhat like waves through water. Some sound waves, such as those we call thunder, are powerful enough to make light objects some distance away shake and rattle.

If we could see sound waves, we would notice that they come in different shapes and sizes. Some are no more than ripples on the surface of a pond. Others are like great ocean waves. As the sound waves are received by an ear, the brain can distinguish what kind they are. There are three different things for the ear and brain to recognize:

- **volume:** how loud the sound is;
- **pitch:** how high or low it is; and
- **tone:** the type or quality of the sound.

The sound waves each object produces are different. This means that two notes played at the same volume and the same pitch on two different musical instruments, for example a flute and a clarinet, will sound quite unlike each other.

The woodwind section of the orchestra is usually in the center, behind the strings and in front of the percussion.

How Woodwind Instruments Work

WHAT IS A WOODWIND INSTRUMENT?

All the instruments called "woodwind" work in the same way. Every woodwind instrument has a tube, or sound pipe, and the player makes the air in the pipe move by blowing into or across one end of it. The sound is made in two ways. This moving air is made to vibrate by being split by the sharp edge of the **mouthpiece** (as in the flute) or it makes a piece of cane called a reed vibrate (as in the clarinet). The vibrations of the reed then make the air in the sound pipe vibrate. Several of the instruments in the woodwind family are actually made of metal or plastic. The oldest instruments in the family were mostly made of wood, horn, or bone.

The material an instrument is made of and the shape, or **profile,** of the sound pipe affect its tone, or **timbre**. It is the combination of material, shape, and the way of making the sound that gives each woodwind instrument its special character. The system used to change the notes also makes the flute different from the clarinet, the clarinet different from the oboe, and so on.

Edge Tone

If you've ever blown across a bottle and made a booming note, you've used **edge tone**. When moving air is split by a sharp edge, the vibrations that occur produce a note. The two commonest types of edge tone are found in the flute (where the player blows across a hole like the top of a bottle) and the recorder (where the player's breath travels down a **duct** at a sharp edge). Sometimes recorders are called "duct-flutes." If you play it by itself, the recorder mouthpiece makes a shrill whistle.

The squawk of a reed or the whistle of edge tone makes the column of air in the instrument's sound pipe vibrate. The longer and wider this **air column** is, the deeper the note. The shorter and thinner it is, the higher the note. A player changes notes by opening or closing holes in the sound pipe. This alters the length of the vibrating column of air inside it. When all the holes are covered, the instrument plays its lowest note. In some instruments, the player's fingers cover the holes, while in others **keys** are used. Certain kinds of keys open and shut holes at the extreme ends of the sound pipe, far beyond the span of the player's hand. This can make the sound pipe very long (for deep sounds) or extremely short (for shrill sounds). When all the holes are open, the air column is at its shortest, and the instrument plays its highest note. If you want to play higher still, you need to build a smaller version of the instrument. Similarly, the only way of going lower than an instrument's lowest note, played with the sound holes shut, is to build a bigger version.

Instrumental families are the result of experiments to reach the highest and lowest extremes of pitch by building instruments in different sizes.

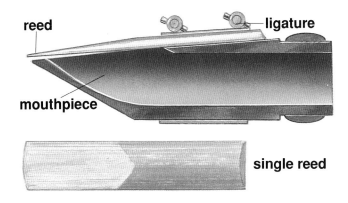

reed   ligature

mouthpiece

single reed

A single reed by itself, and a cross section of it clamped onto a clarinet mouthpiece.

Reeds

There are two types of reeds: single reed, which is a large piece of flat cane, and a double reed, where one flat reed is split into two and then the pieces are tied tightly back together. In both cases the reed vibrates against the lips as the player blows past it into the instrument.

Single reeds are attached to the instrument's mouthpiece with a **ligature**. (The diagram shows how this works.) The player uses saliva to moisten the reed, although a "hard" reed remains stiff, while a "soft" reed is more supple.

If you listened to a single reed clamped to a mouthpiece by its ligature, being blown by itself, it would make an unpleasant squawk. A double reed, which doesn't need to be clamped to a mouthpiece in order to make a noise, makes a ducklike quack when the player blows through it alone.

The double reed of a bassoon. It is cut to shape and a sharp knife is used to adjust its thickness.

The Recorder Family

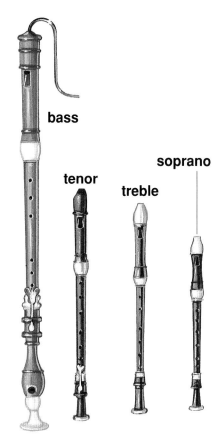

bass

tenor

treble

soprano

The recorder family

The most common recorder is the soprano, or **descant,** recorder, which thousands of children all over the world learn at school. Its original 12th-century ancestors were made of wood. Other early relatives were made of animal bone or horn. Today recorders are usually made of plastic.

At the beginning of the 20th-century the recorder was almost a forgotten instrument. An English instrument builder named Arnold Dolmetsch taught himself how to make recorders from wood when he replaced a lost instrument. It takes a skilled craftsperson a long time to build a wooden recorder, and so these are very expensive. The Dolmetsch factory eventually developed a reliable, in-tune instrument that could be mass-produced in plastic. These are much cheaper, and thousands of people learn the recorder as their first instrument.

Most people learn to play the soprano recorder, but the family has other, less-familiar members in different sizes.

The Soprano Recorder
The soprano recorder is made in three parts. Each is called a **joint**. At the top is the mouthpiece, in the middle (carrying most of the **finger holes**) is the **head joint**, and at the bottom is the **bell**. When the instrument is put together for playing, lightly greased cork rings seal the joints and keep them from leaking air. The recorder can be taken apart for cleaning and storing. The player's left hand covers the three finger holes and thumbhole nearest to the mouthpiece, and the right hand covers the lower holes. The bottom two holes are split, and you can see from the diagram that each is actually two holes. The player learns to cover and uncover half of these split holes at a time. The mouthpiece makes the sound through edge tone.

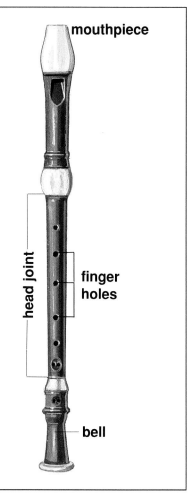

mouthpiece

head joint

finger holes

bell

THE BIGGER RECORDERS

The **treble** and **tenor** recorders are the next two sizes up from the soprano. If a player covers all the holes on the soprano recorder, the note produced is C. Which notes are produced when all the holes are covered on the treble and the tenor instruments?

The Lowest Notes from a Range of Recorders

The lowest note of the treble is F, and the lowest note of the tenor is C — exactly one **octave** lower than the soprano. The lowest note on the tenor is made by covering a hole farther down the instrument than the little finger of the player's right hand can reach. To cover it, the player presses a key that operates a pad over the hole. The bass recorder also has a key and pad. It is built in F like the treble but is so big that the player has to blow into a tube, or **crook**.

SOLO PLAYING

The soprano and treble recorders, with their penetrating tone, were used in early **consorts** or ensembles to play difficult **solo** pieces. The tenor and bass instruments play lower parts, accompanying the melody.

Playing a bass recorder

Recorder Playing

Many schools teach the recorder. It is an easy instrument to learn and is usually taught in groups, where you can discover the fun of playing music with other people. Learning the recorder will help you to read music, and if you spend a small amount of time practicing every day, you will soon develop enough skill to play demanding solos. From the recorder you can easily go on to other woodwind instruments.

Listening Guide

J.S. Bach wrote the "flute" parts in his Brandenburg Concerto No. 4 for recorders. Benjamin Britten used recorders in his "Alpine Suite." Paul Hindemith used them in his trio *Plöner Musiktag*. Many works that have been written for children have included recorder parts.

Unusual Recorders

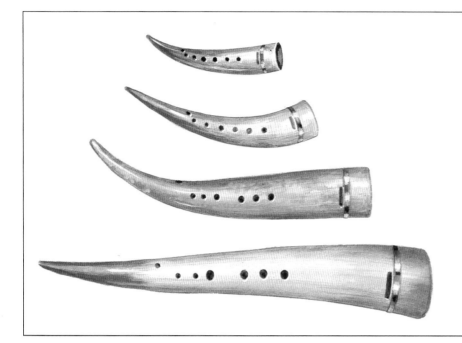

The gëmshorn was a kind of duct flute similar to the recorder made out of the horns of the gemsbok, or chamois. A wooden plug was put into the wide end of the horn, with a small hole, or duct, for the player to blow into. The whistle (or "lip") and all the finger holes were cut into the horn itself. Its quiet tone was charming, and recordings have been made of it by early-music specialists including the well-known player David Munrow.

The *cyla-diare* comes from Albania. It is like two recorders side by side, carved out of a single block of wood. The player plays long continuous notes (**drones**) with the left-hand pipe. The tune is played with the right-hand pipe, which has four or five finger holes.

Perhaps the tiniest duct flute is the picco **pipe** named after a famous 19th-century blind flute player. Picco played a pipe with just two holes on the front and a thumbhole behind. By covering and uncovering the end of the instrument with great skill, he could play several octaves.

The *moseños* from Bolivia is very uncomfortable to play. Players have to hold their heads high to blow into the 35-inch (90-cm) tube and stretch to cover the five finger holes at the bottom of the tube to change the notes.

All over South America, musicians play the *pincullo*. This is a kind of recorder made from cane, wood, and sometimes bone. It varies in length from about 16 inches (40 cm) to a giant 47 inches (120 cm). It is often played at Carnival time. The *pincullo* has three finger holes, so the player can operate them with one hand and play a drum with the other. This is like the old European pipe and tabor, common in the Middle Ages, which is still played in parts of France, Portugal, and Spain. In about 1588, the English actor William Kemp danced from London to Norwich accompanied only by a pipe and tabor player. It took him nine days, and his journey gave us the phrase "a nine days' wonder."

Kemps nine daies vvonder

Performed in a daunce from London to Norwich.

Containing the pleasure, paines and kinde entertainment of *William Kemp* betweene *London* and that Citty in his late Morrice.

Wherein is somewhat set downe worth note; to reprooue the slaunders spred of him: many things merry, nothing hurtfull.

Written by himselfe to satisfie his friends.

LONDON

Printed by *E. A.* for *Nicholas Ling*, and are to be solde at his shop at the west doore of Saint Paules Church. 1600.

A page from William Kemp's booklet about his dance from London to Norwich. His pipe and tabor player was named Thomas Slye.

These *moseños* players from near Lake Titicaca are demonstrating two sizes of this Bolivian instrument, often played at New Year's celebrations.

The Flute Family

All the flute family make their sound by edge tone. The player blows across a hole set at the end of the instrument.

Western concert flutes come in at least four sizes. They are all **transverse** (held out to the right-hand side). The player blows across a hole about 2 inches (5 cm) from the end. The smallest flute is called the piccolo (the Italian word for *small*) and is about 12 inches (30 cm) long. The next biggest is the ordinary flute, which is 24 inches (60 cm) long. The larger members of the family are the **alto** and **bass** flutes.

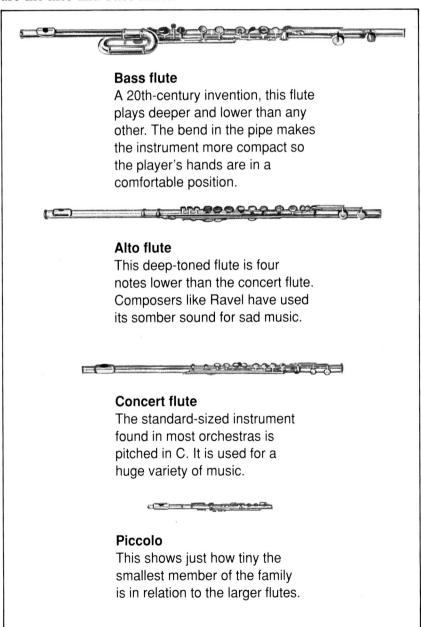

Bass flute
A 20th-century invention, this flute plays deeper and lower than any other. The bend in the pipe makes the instrument more compact so the player's hands are in a comfortable position.

Alto flute
This deep-toned flute is four notes lower than the concert flute. Composers like Ravel have used its somber sound for sad music.

Concert flute
The standard-sized instrument found in most orchestras is pitched in C. It is used for a huge variety of music.

Piccolo
This shows just how tiny the smallest member of the family is in relation to the larger flutes.

The flute family

THE PICCOLO

The shrill sound of the piccolo makes it easy to identify above the sound of an orchestra. It has a higher pitch than the concert flute and is used for display music and special effects.

This piccolo player shows the transverse playing position.

HOLES AND KEYS

The simplest transverse flute is called a fife. It has one hole to blow across and six finger holes. The player's fingers cover the holes and change the length of the sound pipe in the same way as a recorder. The most comfortable position for the player's fingers is not always the best position for the sound holes. For the best tone and **tuning** the holes are sometimes drilled in awkward places. So a system of pads and keys was invented so the player could comfortably open and shut these holes in the sound pipe. The flute has a more complicated set of keys developed by a German inventor, Theobald Boehm. It is known today as the Boehm system.

A flute player in the mid-1600s.

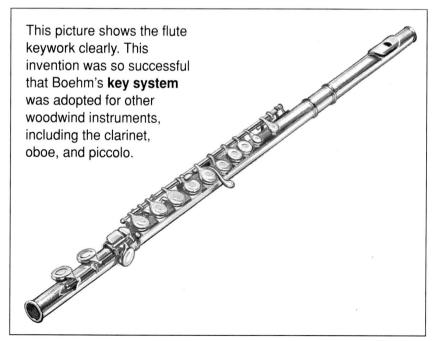

This picture shows the flute keywork clearly. This invention was so successful that Boehm's **key system** was adopted for other woodwind instruments, including the clarinet, oboe, and piccolo.

Flutes from Around the World

This Japanese *ryuteki* player is wearing special ceremonial clothes. The *ryuteki* is used to play the main melody in court and folk music. Like the *nokan,* the *ryuteki* is made of bamboo and has seven finger holes.

In Japan, one transverse flute is called the *nokan*. It has seven finger holes and is made of sections of split bamboo, wrapped in bark and painted. Inside the *nokan* is a metal weight to help the player balance the instrument. The *nokan* is part of the ensemble that plays during *Nö* and *Kabuki* theater performances, which combine dance, mime, music, and melodrama. The *ryuteki* is similar to the *nokan*, but it is used mainly for music in the royal court. Its name comes from a 12th-century Chinese instrument called the dragon flute, which had a fierce dragon's head carved at the end opposite the mouth hole.

In India, paintings from as early as 300 B.C. show flutes being played in courts and temples. Writings in Sanskrit (the ancient language of India) describe the flutes and how they were built and played 1,000 years ago, but in the 12th century, when much of India was under Muslim rule, the flute became less popular. It is now a popular instrument again. The short *venu* is used in the south of the country, and the long bamboo *basuri* is popular in the north.

Panpipes usually come in sets, but in Romania the *tilinca* is like a single panpipe. The player blows over the top of a tube about 24 inches (60 cm) long, changing the notes by covering and uncovering the hole at the other end of the tube. Romanians also play full sets of panpipes called *nai*.

A group from Latin America playing three different sizes of panpipes.

Flute Playing

With most instruments you can make your first sounds quickly and easily. Just learning to blow across the mouthpiece of the flute and produce a note is almost the hardest part of starting to play the instrument. Your first sounds may be odd squeaks or silent rushes of air! Finding a suitable instrument can be quite expensive, and it may help to borrow a flute from a school, college, or youth orchestra to try it out and get started. Hard daily practice is a must, and it helps if you've already learned the recorder. You can play in orchestras, chamber groups, or wind bands.

Listening Guides

Much of the greatest music for the flute was written in the 18th century. J.S. Bach wrote solo flute sonatas and concertos (in which the flute soloist is accompanied by an orchestra), and Handel wrote 12 sonatas. Telemann, Rameau, and Mozart wrote many pieces for the flute.

Twentieth-century composers like Debussy and Ravel have featured the flute in their compositions. In jazz, the flute has been used by Herbie Mann, Hubert Laws, and by the blind multi-instrumentalist Roland Kirk. In rock music, Ian Anderson, the leader of Jethro Tull, is famous for playing the flute.

The Clarinet Family

THE CHALUMEAU

In the late 17th century, instrument makers tried to invent a louder version of the recorder.

A single reed mouthpiece was attached to a pipe with seven finger holes, and the instrument was called the chalumeau. The earliest mouthpieces had the reed on top, so that it vibrated against the player's upper lip. The chalumeau had a loud, strong lower **register**, but players found it very hard to get a range of high notes. The clarinet was developed as instrument builders tried to produce an upper register for the chalumeau.

In the early 18th century, the position of the reed was moved so that it was below the mouthpiece, against the player's bottom lip. The mouthpiece itself had become smaller. Then a new key called the register key was added, opening a hole closer to the top of the instrument. A better mouthpiece and this new key gave the new instrument a much greater range. The chalumeau gradually fell out of use. Today we remember it by calling the lower notes of the clarinet its "chalumeau" register.

This is a modern reconstruction of a chalumeau. The reed is below the mouthpiece and is held in place by a thread ligature.

THE CLARINET

The modern clarinet was invented between 1700 and 1720 by Johann Christoph Denner in Nuremberg, Germany. The first clarinets were very different from the modern clarinet.

More and more keys were gradually added until the instrument looked like the one that is used today. It has a Boehm system of keys, like the flute. You can see from the picture that it is more complex than the recorder.

The instrument most of us think of as a clarinet is the B♭ (B flat) soprano instrument. Over the years, clarinets have been built in a range of sizes, but the most commonly used today are the B♭ and A♭ sopranos, the E♭ sopranino, and the B♭ bass clarinet. The modern bass instrument combines the straight body and keywork of a normal clarinet with a crook and bell similar to a saxophone.

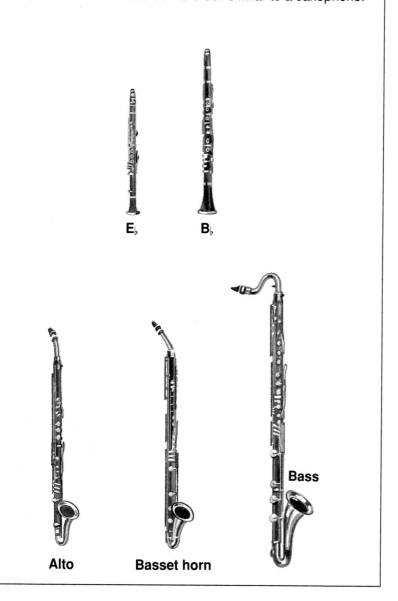

E♭　　**B♭**

Bass

Alto　　**Basset horn**

Emma Johnson playing the B♭ clarinet.

In jazz, there were many players who used the clarinet, for example, Johnny Dodds, Sidney Bechet, Barney Bigard (who played "Barney's Concerto" with Duke Ellington's band), and Benny Goodman, the most technically brilliant of all. Goodman also asked classical composers like Bartók, Copland, and Hindemith to write clarinet pieces for him.

UNUSUAL CLARINETS

Jazz player Adrian Rollini made records using a miniature clarinet called the Hot Fountain Pen. As its name suggests, it was tiny — it could be kept in a suit pocket. It had a shrill squeaky sound and no real keys.

The *nadsip* of Hungary is very similar to Rollini's instrument. It is a tiny clarinet, about the size of a piccolo. Ordinary soprano clarinets are widely used in Hungarian and Romanian gypsy music.

The *launeddas* of Sardinia is made of three simple clarinets bound together. The player has to blow through three reeds at the same time. One pipe has no holes and is just a drone. It and the middle-sized pipe are held in the player's left hand, while the shortest pipe is played with the right hand.

IN THE ORCHESTRA

The woodwind section of a symphony orchestra contains a group of two or three clarinets. The players will use different members of the clarinet family in most performances. Composers use a wide variety of sounds from this section of the woodwinds, and some famous passages from classical music depend on the clarinet, such as parts of Beethoven's "Pastoral Symphony" or Berlioz's *Symphonie fantastique*. Great players include Jack Brymer, Gervase de Peyer, Emma Johnson, and Richard Stoltzman.

The clarinets in the orchestra

Clarinet Playing

The clarinet is held like a treble recorder, and many clarinetists first learned the recorder. Learning to make the single reed work against your lower lip is hard at first, but with even ten minutes of practice a day you will quickly develop the skill.

Clarinetists play in wind bands, orchestras, and as soloists in chamber music. If you master the clarinet you will be able to transfer to the saxophone family. (Turn to page 20 to see the saxophone family.) A plastic clarinet is reasonably cheap to buy, but you also need to buy a supply of reeds.

Listening Guide

In 1791 Mozart wrote his clarinet concerto, which displays the clarinet's brilliant upper register, and its dark lower range. In 1811 Carl Maria Von Weber wrote two concertos, both designed to show the agility of the clarinet. In chamber music (for small groups of instruments) there are pieces by many major composers, including Beethoven and Brahms. Twentieth-century composers like Igor Stravinsky (in his *Ebony Concerto*) and George Gershwin (in *Rhapsody in Blue*) have made use of the instrument.

The Saxophone Family

All the other woodwind instruments in this book developed over time, or were adopted from earlier instruments. The saxophone family was invented as a complete set by one man, Adolphe Sax, in 1846. Saxophones are made of brass, with a conical (cone-shaped) bore, and each has a single reed like a clarinet. The body of the saxophone has between 18 and 20 sound holes, covered by pads. The keys are easy to operate, somewhat like playing the recorder with some parts of the Boehm system added to it.

You can see the family in the diagram below. The soprano is built in two forms, straight (like a thick clarinet) and curved.

KEYS AND PADS

Saxophones are simpler than clarinets. In almost all systems of clarinet fingering, the player's fingers actually cover some of the sound holes. A few of these holes are surrounded by rings that open or close other sound holes on the instrument. Only those holes that are not easily reached by the player's fingers are covered by pads. On the saxophone, even those holes directly under the player's fingers have pads.

Of the 14 different sizes in the complete set of saxophones invented in 1846, only five remain in use today.

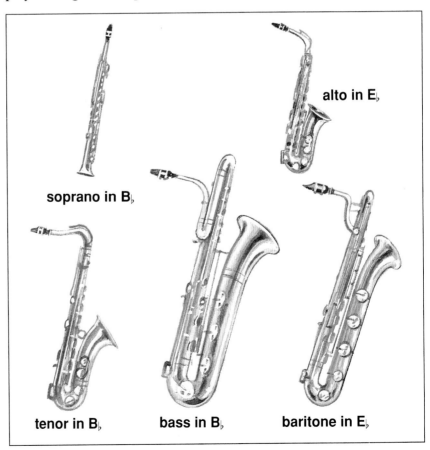

alto in E♭

soprano in B♭

tenor in B♭

bass in B♭

baritone in E♭

THE MOUTHPIECE

Again, saxophones and clarinets are different. The clarinet mouthpiece is designed to fit into the top of the **tuning barrel** of the instrument. The player tunes the instrument by adjusting the joint between the tuning barrel and the head joint. If you look closely at the saxophone family you will see that they do not have tuning barrels. Instead, the mouthpiece fits over the top of the instrument. In the case of the tenor, **baritone**, and bass saxophones, the mouthpiece fits over a crook that extends the top of the saxophone toward the player's mouth, just like the bass recorder. The player tunes the saxophone by adjusting the position of the mouthpiece.

Jazz

It is in jazz that the saxophone has become most important. In almost all styles and periods of jazz, all members of the family have been used. Big bands, like those of Duke Ellington and Count Basie, used a section of four saxophones — an alto, two tenors, and a baritone. Tenor soloists like Coleman Hawkins and Lester Young came from the big bands. Sidney Bechet and his pupils used the soprano instrument. Charlie Parker developed his breathtaking style of modern jazz on the alto. More recently, young jazz musicians have been influenced by the tenor playing of John Coltrane and Sonny Rollins. Players like Ralph Moore, Steve Williamson, Courtney Pine, and Branford Marsalis are becoming new stars of the saxophone.

Courtney Pine plays tenor sax.

Unusual Saxophones

Investors and instrument builders have designed many additions to Sax's original family of instruments. One of the strangest is the slide saxophone, which is the same size as the soprano instrument but is operated by a kind of trombone slide. American jazzman Snub Mosley made this instrument famous, becoming known as "the man with the funny horn."

Multi-instrumentalist Roland Kirk played several saxophones at once. Although he was blind, he could play with remarkable agility on a forest of instruments slung around his neck. He used two very unusual kinds of saxophones, the manzello which was a slightly curved soprano, and the stritch which was a straightened-out version of the alto.

The bass saxophone is big, cumbersome, and difficult to handle. It is seldom used, except in place of the double bass or tuba in 1920s dance music. As one of the most unusual instruments of all, it has received a lot of unexpected attention. Novels have been written about it, television films have been made about it, and rock star Andy "Thunderclap" Newman used to take one everywhere.

Roland Kirk with his collection of unusual saxophones.

Saxophone Playing

Most professional saxophonists play all members of the family. When you start to play, you'll start on the alto or tenor. The saxophone is surprisingly like a recorder, and the fingering is very similar. The feel of the mouthpiece is also very similar to that of the clarinet.

Because all the pads and springs need to be in good working order, a saxophone can be expensive to maintain. Borrow one from a school or college to learn the basics. You'll be able to play rock or jazz if you practice every day.

Listening Guide

Some composers have written saxophone concertos, and others have written chamber music for the saxophone quartet. To hear some of the best music for the instrument, find Coleman Hawkins playing "Body and Soul," Lester Young playing "Lester Leaps In," or any of the recordings of Charlie Parker. More recent recordings have been made by Bobby Watson, Christopher Hollyday, Phil Woods, Steve Williamson, and Paul Desmond of the Dave Brubeck Quartet.

The Oboe

The name *oboe* comes from the French word *hautbois*, which means "high-" or "loud-wood." In the Middle Ages, there were similar instruments that had a brash, trumpetlike sound. One of the most common of these was the shawm. Although the shawm has a kind of wooden cup around the reed called a "pirouette," it works in much the same way as an oboe and has a harsh sound.

The present-day oboe was developed from the shawm by Jean Hotteterre in the 17th-century French court. The larger members of the oboe family in alto or tenor pitch have a bulbous egg-shaped bell. The most commonly used of these are the alto oboe d'amore in A, and the English horn or *cor anglais* in F.

The oboe has not been widely used in jazz or rock music. In the 1930s, Alec Wilder composed an oboe concerto for popular bandleader Mitch Miller, and jazz player Karl Jenkins played it in groups led by Graham Collier and Ian Carr.

Shawms being played in a 16th-century Flemish procession. In Catalonia, Spain, the shawm is still used in the *cobla* bands that accompany the region's famous *sardana* dances.

The three main sections of an oboe and (right) the oboe's double reed.

upper joint

keys

reed

lower joint

staple

bell joint

The body of the oboe looks somewhat like a clarinet. It is generally built of dark wood or plastic and has Boehm system keys. The normal orchestral instrument is pitched in C. The main difference between the oboe and the clarinet is in the way it makes a sound. The oboe uses a double reed, and this fits in the top of the instrument on its **staple**. The ends of the double reed are placed between the player's lips and vibrate as the player blows. The oboe plays the note that the whole orchestra uses when it tunes up.

THE HECKELPHONE

This baritone version of the oboe was invented in 1904 by William Heckel. Other large oboes had a quiet tone, and Heckel developed an instrument that would be stronger. It has a large double reed connected to the instrument by a curved metal **crook**. Richard Strauss featured the instrument in his opera *Salome*, and many composers have written for the heckelphone. It is sometimes used as a substitute for other large oboes.

Listening Guide

Handel wrote a set of three concertos for the oboe. Vivaldi and Albinoni also wrote for the oboe. J.S. Bach used it to accompany the singers in his religious compositions. This kind of solo is called an "obbligato." After 1750 the oboe became part of the orchestra, and many composers including Mozart, Beethoven, Schubert, Brahms, and Mahler have used it.

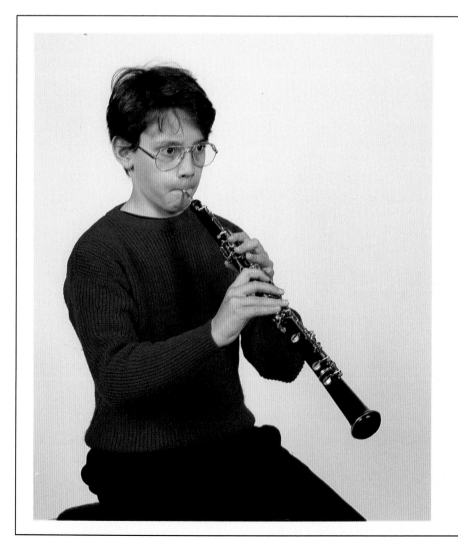

Oboe Playing

Because oboes have Boehm system keys, the fingering is similar to the clarinet and flute. You will need to practice for a short time every day as controlling the double reed is difficult. No two reeds are the same, and they can sometimes be very temperamental. Some squeak; others do not produce a note easily. The hardest part of learning to play the oboe is controlling the reed.

If you want to play classical orchestral or chamber music, the oboe is a good choice. Oboes are quite expensive to buy, so it is a good idea to borrow one to learn the basics.

The Bassoon

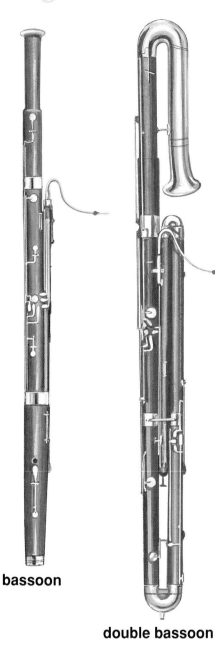

The bassoon is the bass member of the woodwind family. It has a double reed and is a modern version of an early instrument called the dulcian, or curtall. These early bassoons were made from one piece of wood rather than in separate joints. Dulcians were made in sets or consorts, with tiny treble or descant versions, but the most common dulcian was the middle-sized instrument. The bassoon's sound pipe doubles back on itself like a bent stick.

By the early 17th century, French instrument makers had developed the modern bassoon from the dulcian and from an instrument made by Afranio in about 1520 called the phagotus. At first, the bassoon had few keys. Because it had a very long sound pipe and only a few finger holes, its range was small and it was difficult to play in tune.

Instrument makers have tried over the years to improve the bassoon by arranging keys to fit the player's hand. Two systems have become most popular, the French (made by Buffet) and the German (made by Heckel).

bassoon

double bassoon

Two bassoon players in the woodwind section of an orchestra

Bassoon Playing

The bassoon (like the double bass) is a large instrument. You need to be big enough to reach the finger holes, and your hand needs to stretch to cover them all.

It is a heavy instrument that is supported on a string around the player's neck. The bassoon's double reed is somewhat easier to control than the oboe's.

Because of its size, the bassoon is expensive. It requires regular practice, but once you have learned the basics, you can play a wide range of music.

Listening guide

Mozart's "Bassoon Concerto" was written in 1774 for an early version of the instrument. It is still the most important solo composition written for the bassoon.

Following Mozart's example, many other composers have written concertos for the bassoon, including Elgar and Villa-Lobos. There are smaller "concertantes" by Richard Strauss and Hindemith. The instrument has been widely used in chamber music. Mozart wrote duets for bassoon and cello, and a wind quintet (for oboe, clarinet, horn, bassoon, and piano). Ludwig van Beethoven wrote a number of pieces for wind ensemble, such as his famous octet of 1792, which includes two bassoons.

Other Woodwind Instruments

Listening Guide
Composers like Vaughan Williams and Milhaud wrote for the harmonica, and Malcolm Arnold has even written a full-scale concerto for it.

One group of instruments that do not appear in the symphony orchestra use a **free reed** to make their sound. Free reeds do not vibrate against a player's lips like the single reed of the clarinet and saxophone, or the double reed of the bassoon and oboe. Instead, free reeds make a sound as air passes through them, and they do not all depend on a player's breath for a supply of air.

The harmonica, or mouth organ, depends on the player's breath, but many other free reed instruments use **bellows** of some sort to supply the air to their reeds. These include the bagpipes, as well as the families of concertinas and accordions.

THE HARMONICA

The harmonica is a straighforward instrument, with a set of free reeds in a metal case. The notes of the scale can be played by alternately breathing in and out, and a surprising range of music has been written for it. The instrument has a number of **virtuoso** players, including Larry Adler and Belgian jazzman "Toots" Thielemans. It is also important in the blues. In Chicago, Illinois, where it was played by Junior Wells and Sonny Terry, it was nicknamed the "blues harp."

Harmonica Playing
The harmonica is cheap to buy. Simple mouth organs do not have the full range of notes, but more complicated instruments are built to professional standards.

Harmonicas are portable, and you can play them anywhere, but they are quite hard to play with other instruments until you are fairly proficient. But harmonica bands have been popular in the U.S.

THE BAGPIPES

The Scottish bagpipes are perhaps the best known of a huge family of different types of pipes from around the world. The *musette* and *cornemuse* from France, the *gaita* from Spain, the *bock* from Germany, and the *dudy* from Czechoslovakia, not to mention the *uilleann* pipes from Ireland, are all varieties of the same instrument. There are many recordings of all these instruments, playing folk, dance, and ceremonial music. All of these instruments contain sets of free reed pipes, blown by a bag or bellows that is generally inflated through a mouthpiece and squeezed under the player's arm to force air into the pipes. Usually, only one of the pipes, called the **chanter**, has finger holes. It is this pipe that is used to play a melody. The other pipes play long, continuous notes and are called **drones**.

Bagpipes Playing

Controlling the bag, the airflow, the drones, and the chanter is very difficult, sort of like fighting an octopus! Players first learn to finger melodies on the chanter in the same way as the recorder. Then they learn to blow up the bag and direct the air into the pipes. There are pipe bands in many parts of the world, and to complicate matters more, these players have to learn to march in step while playing the same notes at the same time!

THE ACCORDION AND THE CONCERTINA

Both these instruments have sets of free reeds mounted in keyboards between which are a set of bellows. In the accordion, there are usually two keyboards: piano keys for the right hand, which play a melody, and sets of buttons for the left, which sound accompanying chords. The concertina (invented in 1829 by Sir Charles Wheatstone) has two sets of buttons, one on each end of the bellows, and it fits more neatly into the player's hands than the larger and more powerful accordion.

Here you can see the treble (piano) keyboard on the left and the bass (button) keyboard on the right, with the bellows in the middle.

29

Glossary

air column   length of air in the pipe, which can be shortened by opening sound holes

alto   lower range of notes sung by a female voice

baritone   medium range of notes sung by an adult male voice

bass   lowest range of notes sung by an adult male voice

bell   flared opening at the opposite end of a woodwind instrument from the mouthpiece

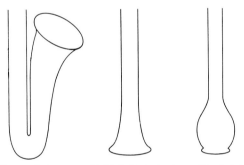

bass clarinet   B♭ (B flat) clarinet   English horn

bellows   pump used to direct air into the sound pipes of free reed instruments

chanter   pipe on a bagpipe that carries the finger holes

consort   group of several players performing together (The modern word "concert" means almost the same thing.)

crook   bent metal tube joining the top of the main sound pipe and the mouthpiece

descant   another name used for the soprano recorder

drone   pipe and free reed that makes a continuous single note in a bagpipe

duct   whistle mouthpiece that directs air onto a sharp edge and splits it

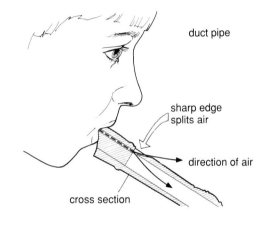

duct pipe

sharp edge splits air

direction of air

cross section

edge tone   sound that results from the vibrations of air split when it hits a sharp edge (see page 6)

ensemble   a group of instrumental players

finger hole   sound hole that is controlled by the pad of a player's finger

free reed   reed, usually made of metal, that is fastened only at one end

head joint   section nearest to the player

joint   one of the separate parts of a woodwind instrument

key	a lever with a spring that operates a pad over a sound hole at one end and is worked by the player's finger at the other
key system	the mechanism that allows the player to open and shut holes in the sound pipe using keys and pads
ligature	the clamp that holds a single reed onto a clarinet or saxophone mouthpiece
mouthpiece	the section of an instrument the player blows into or across
octave	eight notes of a complete scale
pipe	tube of a wind instrument, and the name of a three-hole edge tone instrument played together with a simple drum or "tabor"
pitch	the level of a note, indicated by its position on the scale
profile	cross section of an instrument
register	a part of the sound range of an instrument
solo	piece of music played or sung by one person
soprano	highest range of notes sung by a female or young male voice
staple	the tube to which the double reed of an oboe or bassoon is attached

tenor	highest range of notes sung by an adult male voice
timbre	characteristic quality of sound produced by a particular instrument
tone	how clear a sound is
transverse flute	flute played crosswise (held out to the right-hand side)

transverse flute

player blows across mouthpiece

direction of air

treble	range of notes sung by the highest boy's voice, equivalent to soprano
tuning	making an instrument ready to play the correct pitch
tuning barrel	section between the mouthpiece and head joint
virtuoso	someone especially skilled at playing a particular instrument
volume	the loudness or softness of a sound

Index